THE YOUNG BILLIONAIRE

THE PRICE OF AMBITION

CWEBILE NDEBELE (BILLIONAIRE SPIKES)

To dreamers and believers everywhere,

This book is dedicated to those who dare to chase their dreams, no matter the obstacles in their path. To the ones who believe in the power of friendship, love, and resilience to overcome even the darkest of nights. May your journey be filled with hope, courage, and the unwavering determination to never give up on the dreams that set your soul on fire.

With love and gratitude,

Cwebile Ndebele (B.S)

Contents

Foreword

In "The Young Billionaire," **Cwebile Ndebele** *invites readers into a world where ambition and adversity collide, and where the bonds of friendship and love are tested in the crucible of success. Through the captivating tale of Billy and his companions,* **Mr.Ndebele** *explores the complexities of wealth, power, and the pursuit of dreams, weaving a narrative that is as poignant as it is exhilarating.*

As you embark on this journey, prepare to be swept away by the vibrant streets of Mumbai, the dynamic characters who inhabit them, and the timeless themes of resilience, redemption, and the indomitable human spirit. "The Young Billionaire" is not just a story; it is an exploration of what it means to be truly wealthy, in heart and in soul.

So, dear reader, let yourself be immersed in the pages that follow, and allow the world of Billy and his friends to capture your imagination and ignite your spirit. For in their story lies a reminder that no dream is too big, no obstacle too daunting, and no journey too perilous when embarked upon with courage, determination, and the unwavering belief in the power of love and friendship.

Cwebile Ndebele (B.S)

Preface

In the pages that follow, you will embark on a journey into the heart of Mumbai—a city teeming with life, ambition, and the promise of dreams fulfilled. Through the eyes of Billy and his companions, you will witness the highs and lows of the human experience, the triumphs and tribulations of chasing success, and the enduring power of love and friendship to light the way through even the darkest of nights.

As the author of "The Young Billionaire," I am honored to share this story with you, dear reader. It is a tale born from my own fascination with the intricacies of the human spirit, and my belief in the transformative power of storytelling to inspire, uplift, and connect us all.

In writing this novel, my hope is not only to entertain, but to offer a glimpse into a world where dreams are within reach, and where the bonds of friendship and love are the truest measure of wealth. So, as you turn the pages and lose yourself in the adventures of Billy and his friends, I invite you to open your heart to the possibility of new beginnings, and to embrace the journey with courage, compassion, and an unwavering belief in the power of dreams.

With deepest gratitude,
Cwebile Ndebele (B.S)

Acknowledgements

Writing a novel is not a solitary endeavor, and "The Young Billionaire" would not have been possible without the support, guidance, and encouragement of countless individuals along the way.

*First and foremost, I would like to express my heartfelt gratitude to my mother [**Elitha Sibanda**], my father [**Artwel Ndebele**] and the family at-large for their unwavering belief in my dreams and their endless love and support. Their encouragement has been my greatest source of strength throughout this journey.*

*I am also deeply indebted to my co-authors [**Kupakwashe Mutsvedu, Diana Mapfumo and vimbainashe Mararira**] and friends, whose laughter, companionship, and unwavering faith in my abilities have kept me going through the highs and lows of the writing process. Your friendship means the world to me.*

A special thank you to my editor and beta readers for their invaluable feedback and insight, which helped shape this story into the polished gem it is today. Your dedication and passion for storytelling are truly inspiring.

*I would also like to extend my thanks to the team at [**Notion Press**], whose professionalism, expertise, and unwavering commitment to excellence have made this book a reality.*

Last but not least, to you, dear reader, thank you for embarking on this journey with me. Your support means more than words can express, and I hope that "The Young Billionaire" brings you as much joy and inspiration as it has brought me.

With deepest appreciation,

Cwebile Ndebele (B.S)

Prologue

In the sprawling metropolis of Mumbai, where dreams are born and fortunes are made, a tale of ambition, love, and betrayal unfolds. It is a story that begins with a young man named Billy, whose journey from rags to riches is a testament to the power of determination and the pursuit of dreams.

But behind the glitz and glamour of Billy's success lies a world of secrets and shadows, where friendships are tested, loyalties are questioned, and the price of ambition may prove higher than anyone could have imagined.

As we step into the world of "The Young Billionaire," we are invited to witness the twists and turns of fate that will shape the destinies of our protagonists. From the bustling streets of Mumbai to the towering heights of success, the journey that lies ahead is one filled with excitement, danger, and the unyielding pursuit of the truth.

So come, dear reader, and join us on this exhilarating adventure into the heart of one of the world's most dynamic cities. For in the pages that follow, you will discover a world where dreams come true, love conquers all, and the bonds of friendship are tested like never before.

Welcome to "The Young Billionaire."

Cwebile Ndebele (B.S)

CHAPTER ONE

<u>SERENDIPITOUS ENCOUNTERS</u>

In the bustling streets of Mumbai, where the vibrant colours of life danced amidst the chaotic symphony of sounds, Billy stood tall, a beacon of youth and ambition. At the tender age of 20, he had already carved his name into the annals of success as a billionaire entrepreneur from Zimbabwe.

It was during his time in India, amidst the corridors of academia and the labyrinth of real estate ventures, that Billy forged a bond with TeaBag, a charismatic Black American millionaire. Their friendship blossomed on the soccer fields, where they spent countless hours chasing dreams and goals, both on and off the pitch.

TeaBag was a man of charm and wit, yet there was one woman who eluded his grasp – Anna. Despite his confidence with the opposite sex, Anna remained a puzzle he couldn't solve. She possessed a fire that intrigued him, a spirit that refused to be tamed by his usual charms. Though Anna harboured her feelings for TeaBag, she hesitated to reveal them, caught in the delicate dance of desire and uncertainty.

Meanwhile, in Billy's world, Stacy reigned as his girlfriend, a beacon of light in the whirlwind of his success. But amidst the glittering facade of their romance, a shadow loomed in the form of Milly, Billy's classmate harbouring a secret crush. Her jealousy simmered beneath a veneer of false smiles, threatening to boil over at any moment.

As the threads of fate intertwined, Stanley emerged as the steady hand guiding Billy's empire, the manager of Billionaire Spikes Housing. With unwavering loyalty and a shrewd mind for business, Stanley stood as the pillar of support amidst the tumultuous currents of success and ambition.

Then came Perfect, the comedic relief in Billy's world, a reminder of the humble beginnings from which he had risen. With laughter as his currency and dreams as his compass, Perfect stood by Billy's side, his unwavering faith a testament to the power of friendship.

In the maze of love and ambition, where dreams collided and hearts intertwined, the story of The Young Billionaire began, its pages unfurling with each heartbeat, its ending as infinite as the stars that adorned the night sky. For in the world of Billy and his companions, anything was possible, and love knew no bounds.

CHAPTER TWO

A SPARK IGNITES

As the sun dipped below the horizon, casting a golden hue over the city skyline, Billy found himself lost in thought, perched on the balcony of his luxurious penthouse. The rhythmic pulse of Mumbai echoed in the distance, a reminder of the vibrant tapestry of life that enveloped him.

TeaBag wandered into the room, his easy smile enlightened by the soft glow of twilight. "Hey, buddy," he said, clapping Billy on the back. "What's on your mind?"

Billy sighed, his gaze drifting to the bustling streets below. "Just thinking about everything," he replied. "The company, Stacy, Milly... It's a lot to juggle."

TeaBag nodded in understanding, his expression sympathetic. "I hear you, man. But don't forget to make time for yourself too. You can't pour from an empty cup."

Billy chuckled, appreciating the wisdom in his friend's words. "Thanks, TeaBag. You always know what to say."

Their conversation was interrupted by the sound of laughter echoing from the living room. Curious, Billy and TeaBag made their way inside to find Perfect holding court, regaling Stacy and Milly with his latest antics.

"Ah, the man of the hour!" Perfect exclaimed, spotting Billy's entrance. "Join us, won't you? I was just telling these lovely ladies about the time I mistook a cactus for a pillow!"

Stacy giggled, her eyes sparkling with amusement. "You never fail to entertain us, Perfect."

Milly forced a smile, though a hint of jealousy flickered in her eyes. "Yes, quite the comedian," she muttered under her breath.

Billy sensed the tension and moved to diffuse it with a smile. "Well, Perfect, you never cease to amaze us with your comedic genius. Truly, you're one of a kind."

Perfect beamed at the praise, puffing out his chest with pride. "Why, thank you, Billy! Coming from you, that means a lot."

As the evening wore on, laughter filled the air, temporarily banishing the shadows of doubt and insecurity that lingered in the corners of Billy's mind. For in moments like these, surrounded by friends who had become family, he knew that no challenge was insurmountable, no obstacle too daunting.

As the stars twinkled overhead, casting their benevolent gaze upon the world below, a spark ignited in Billy's heart, illuminating the path ahead with the promise of new beginnings and endless possibilities.

CHAPTER THREE

THE DANCE OF FATE

Days turned into weeks, and weeks into months, each passing moment a testament to the inevitable march of time. In the heart of Mumbai, amidst the chaos of life and the whispers of destiny, the lives of Billy and his companions continued to intertwine in unexpected ways.

One fateful evening, Billy found himself attending a lavish charity gala, the air thick with the scent of opulence and the murmur of whispered conversations. Dressed in his finest attire, he mingled effortlessly with the elite crowd, his every movement exuding an air of confidence and sophistication.

As the night wore on, Billy's gaze fell upon Anna, her presence captivating him like a moth drawn to a flame. Clad in an elegant gown that shimmered like starlight against her ebony skin, she moved with grace and poise, a vision of beauty that took his breath away.

Unable to resist the pull of fate, Billy made his way across the crowded ballroom, his heart pounding with anticipation. "Anna," he said, his voice barely above a whisper. "You look stunning tonight."

Anna's eyes met his, a hint of surprise flashing in their depths before being replaced by a warm smile. "Thank you, Billy," she replied, her voice soft and melodic. "You clean up rather nicely yourself."

Their conversation flowed effortlessly, each word a thread weaving the tapestry of their connection. As the night wore on, Billy found himself drawn to Anna in ways he had never imagined possible, her laughter a symphony that echoed in his soul.

Meanwhile, across the room, TeaBag found himself locked in a heated debate with Stacy, their voices rising above the din of the crowd. "I'm telling you, TeaBag, you need to make a move on Anna," Stacy insisted, her eyes flashing with determination. "Life's too short to let love pass you by."

TeaBag sighed, running a hand through his hair in frustration. "I know, I know," he muttered, his gaze drifting to where Anna and Billy stood lost in conversation. "But what if she doesn't feel the same way?"

Stacy placed a reassuring hand on his arm, her touch grounding him amid his doubts. "You'll never know unless you try," she said, her voice gentle yet firm. "Trust me, TeaBag. Love has a funny way of surprising us when we least expect it."

And so, amidst the ebb and flow of the evening, the dance of fate continued unabated, each step bringing Billy and Anna closer together, while TeaBag grappled with his feelings of uncertainty and longing. For in the maze of love and desire, where hearts beat as one and dreams took flight on wings of hope, anything was possible. As the night faded into dawn, the promise of tomorrow beckoned, its secrets waiting to be revealed in the light of a new day.

CHAPTER FOUR

<u>THE UNRAVELLING</u>

In the hazy light of dawn, Billy found himself lost in thought, the events of the previous evening swirling in his mind like a tempestuous whirlwind. The memory of his conversation with Anna lingered, a tantalizing glimpse of what could be if only he dared to reach out and seize it.

As he sipped his morning coffee, lost in contemplation, a knock on the door roused him from his dream. With a sigh, he rose from his seat and made his way to answer it, his heart pounding with anticipation.

To his surprise, TeaBag stood on the other side, a troubled expression etched upon his features. "TeaBag, what brings you here so early?" Billy asked, concern lacing his voice.

TeaBag hesitated for a moment before speaking, his words weighed down by the burden of his emotions. "Billy, I need to talk to you about something," he said, his voice tinged with uncertainty. "It's about Anna."

Billy's heart skipped a beat at the mention of her name, a wave of apprehension washing over him like a tidal wave. "What about Anna?" he asked, his voice barely above a whisper.

TeaBag took a deep breath, steeling himself for what was to come. "I think... I think I'm in love with her," he confessed, his words heavy with emotion. "But I don't know what to do. I've never felt this way about anyone before."

Billy's mind reeled at the revelation, his feelings for Anna suddenly thrown into sharp relief. "TeaBag, I... I don't know what to say," he stammered, his thoughts a tangled mess of confusion and desire.

As they stood there, grappling with the weight of their emotions, a sense of inevitability settled over them like a shroud. For in matters of the heart, there were no easy answers, no clear-cut solutions. As the morning sun cast its golden rays upon the world below, Billy and TeaBag found themselves at a crossroads, their destinies intertwined in ways they could never have imagined.

Meanwhile, across the city, Anna sat alone in her apartment, her thoughts consumed by the events of the previous evening. The memory of her conversation with Billy lingered as a bittersweet reminder of the connection they shared, the undeniable spark that ignited between them.

But amidst the chaos of her emotions, a single question lingered, its answer eluding her grasp like a whisper in the wind. For in the depths of her heart, Anna knew that love was a delicate dance, a fragile balance between desire and destiny. As she gazed out at the city below, her heart heavy with longing, she wondered what the future held in store, and whether she dared to leap into the unknown.

CHAPTER FIVE

<u>CROSSROADS OF LOVE</u>

As the sun dipped below the horizon, casting a golden glow over the city of Mumbai, Billy found himself standing at a crossroads, his heart torn between loyalty to his friend and the pull of his desires.

TeaBag's confession weighed heavily on his mind, the weight of it pressing down upon him like a burden too heavy to bear. Yet, amidst the tumult of his emotions, there was a glimmer of hope, a whisper of possibility that danced on the edges of his consciousness.

With a heavy heart, Billy sought solace in the quiet of his penthouse, the silence offering a respite from the chaos of his thoughts. As he stared out at the twinkling lights of the city below, he found himself struggling with the age-old question of love and loyalty, unsure of which path to choose.

Meanwhile, across town, Anna found herself lost in a maze of uncertainty, her heart torn between two men who held sway over her emotions. The memory of her conversation with Billy lingered, a tantalizing glimpse of the connection they shared, while TeaBag's confession echoed in the recesses of her mind, a reminder of the bond they had forged.

With a sigh, Anna retreated into the solitude of her apartment, the walls closing in around her like a prison of her own making. As she wrestled with the complexities of her heart, she knew that a decision loomed on the horizon, one that would irrevocably alter the course of her destiny.

As the night wore on, the city slept beneath a blanket of stars, unaware of the drama unfolding in its midst. Amidst the quietude of the night, Billy and Anna found themselves standing on the precipice of something new, their hearts poised on the edge of a precipice, ready to leap into the unknown.

For in the labyrinth of love and desire, where paths converged and destinies entwined, there were no easy answers, no clear-cut solutions. As the first light of dawn broke over the horizon, illuminating the world in its golden glow, Billy and Anna knew that they stood at the crossroads of love, their fates intertwined in ways they could never have imagined.

CHAPTER SIX

<u>EMBRACING DESTINY</u>

The morning sun rose over Mumbai, painting the sky with hues of orange and pink as the city stirred to life. In Billy's penthouse, the air was heavy with anticipation, the weight of unspoken words lingering between him and Anna like a veil of uncertainty.

As Billy sat at the breakfast table, his thoughts consumed by the events of the previous night, a sense of determination washed over him like a tidal wave. He knew that he couldn't ignore the pull of his heart any longer, couldn't deny the feelings that had taken root within him like a seed planted in fertile soil.

With a resolute nod, Billy rose from his seat, his decision made. Today, he would confront his feelings head-on and would lay bare his heart for all to see. For he knew that life was too short to live in the shadows, too precious to waste on regret and doubt.

Meanwhile, across town, Anna found herself lost in a whirlwind of emotions, her mind a tumultuous sea of conflicting desires. The memory of her conversation with Billy haunted her, a constant reminder of the connection they shared, while TeaBag's confession lingered like a spectre in the recesses of her mind.

With a sigh, Anna resolved to face her feelings head-on, to confront the truth that lay buried beneath layers of fear and uncertainty. For she knew that the heart was a fickle thing, capable of leading us down paths we never imagined possible if only we dared to listen.

As the day wore on, Billy and Anna found themselves drawn together by an invisible thread, their paths converging in ways they could never have predicted. As they stood face to face, the air between them crackling with tension, they knew that the moment of truth had arrived.

"Billy," Anna began, her voice trembling with emotion. "There's something I need to tell you."

But before she could continue, Billy reached out and took her hand in his, his touch sending a jolt of electricity coursing through her veins. "Anna," he said, his voice soft yet firm. "I know what you're going to say, and I want you to know that I feel the same way."

Anna's heart skipped a beat at his words, her breath catching in her throat as tears welled in her eyes. "Billy," she whispered, her voice barely above a whisper. "I... I never thought..."

But Billy silenced her with a kiss, a gentle yet passionate embrace that spoke volumes more than words ever could. As they lost themselves in each other's arms, the world around them faded into obscurity, leaving only the two of them alone in their newfound love.

Meanwhile, across town, TeaBag found himself grappling with his own emotions, his heart heavy with the weight of unspoken words. As he wandered the streets of Mumbai, lost in thought, he couldn't shake the feeling that something had shifted, that the world around him was no longer as it seemed.

With a heavy sigh, TeaBag made his way to a nearby park, seeking solace in the quietude of nature. As he sat beneath the shade of a sprawling tree, the rustling of leaves a soothing lullaby, he knew that he had a choice to make.

For in matters of the heart, there were no easy answers, no clear-cut solutions. As TeaBag closed his eyes and let the gentle breeze wash over him, he knew that he had to follow his heart, no matter where it might lead.

As the sun set over Mumbai, casting long shadows across the cityscape, Billy and Anna found themselves standing on the balcony of his penthouse, their hands intertwined as they gazed out at the twinkling lights below.

"I never imagined that I could feel this way," Anna said, her voice soft yet resolute. "But now that I'm here, with you, I wouldn't change a thing."

Billy smiled, his heart overflowing with love and gratitude. "Neither would I," he replied, pulling her close. "Because this is where I'm meant to be, with you, now and always."

As they watched the stars twinkle overhead, their love shining brighter than any constellation in the night sky, Billy and Anna knew that they had found their happily ever after, their destinies entwined in a love that would endure for all eternity.

CHAPTER SEVEN

NAVIGATING THE UNKNOWN

The days turned into weeks, and the weeks into months, as Billy and Anna embarked on a journey into the unknown, their love blossoming like a flower in the warmth of spring. Each moment spent together was a treasure, a testament to the strength of their bond and the depth of their connection.

As they navigated the highs and lows of their burgeoning relationship, Billy and Anna found solace in each other's arms, their love a beacon of hope in a world filled with uncertainty. Yet, amidst the dizzying whirl of emotions, a shadow loomed on the horizon, threatening to cast a pall over their newfound happiness.

It began with whispers, and murmurs of discontent that spread like wildfire through the corridors of Billionaire Spikes Housing. Rumours swirled about Billy and Anna's relationship, their clandestine romance the subject of gossip and speculation among the company's employees.

At first, Billy paid little heed to the chatter, dismissing it as the idle gossip of jealous tongues. But as the whispers grew louder and more persistent, he couldn't help but feel a twinge of unease gnawing at the edges of his consciousness.

One evening, as Billy sat in his office poring over reports, Stanley entered the room with a troubled expression etched upon his features. "Billy, we need to talk," he said, his voice grave.

Billy looked up from his work, concern furrowing his brow. "What's wrong, Stanley? Is everything alright?"

Stanley hesitated for a moment before speaking, his words weighed down by the gravity of the situation. "It's about the rumours, Billy," he began, his voice tinged with concern. "They're starting to affect morale among the employees. Some of them are even questioning your judgment as CEO."

Billy's heart sank at the revelation, a sense of betrayal coursing through him like a dagger to the heart. He had worked tirelessly to build Billionaire Spikes Housing into a thriving company, pouring his blood, sweat, and tears into every project, only to have it all called into question by baseless gossip.

With a heavy sigh, Billy rose from his seat, his mind racing with thoughts of how to quell the rumours before they spiralled out of control. "Thank you for bringing this to my attention, Stanley," he said, his voice tinged with resignation. "I'll handle it."

So, with a heavy heart and a determination born of necessity, Billy set out to confront the whispers head-on, determined to protect not only his company's reputation but also the fragile peace he had found in Anna's arms.

Meanwhile, across town, Anna found herself grappling with her demons, her insecurities bubbling to the surface like a dormant volcano awakened from its slumber. The weight of the rumours bore down upon her like a crushing weight, threatening to suffocate her beneath its oppressive gaze.

With each passing day, Anna felt herself retreating further into herself, her confidence shaken and her spirit bruised. She knew that she should confide in Billy, and share her fears and doubts with him, but the words caught in her throat like a lump of coal, choking off her ability to speak.

And so, she suffered in silence, her smile a facade masking the turmoil raging within her soul. For she feared that if she were to reveal the depths of her despair, she would only push Billy further away, driving a wedge between them that could never be repaired.

As the days stretched into weeks, Billy and Anna found themselves drifting apart, their once unbreakable bond fraying at the edges like a threadbare garment worn thin by the passage of time. As they stood on the precipice of uncertainty, neither knowing how to bridge the chasm that separated them, they realized that their love was facing its greatest test yet.

But amidst the darkness, a glimmer of hope shone like a beacon in the night sky, a reminder that even in the darkest of times, there was still light to be found. As Billy and Anna clung to that flicker of hope, they knew that no matter what trials lay ahead, they would face them together, hand in hand, hearts entwined in a love that could weather any storm.

As the weight of uncertainty hung heavy in the air, Billy and Anna found themselves caught in a web of doubt and fear, their once-solid foundation shaken to its core. Each passing day brought with it a new wave of challenges, testing the limits of their love and resilience.

Despite Billy's efforts to quell the rumours surrounding their relationship, the whispers persisted, spreading like wildfire through the halls of Billionaire Spikes Housing. As the tension within the company reached a fever pitch, Billy found himself grappling with the realization that his personal life was threatening to overshadow his professional achievements.

Determined to put an end to the speculation once and for all, Billy called for an emergency meeting with the company's executives. As they gathered in the boardroom, the air crackled with tension, each person acutely aware of the gravity of the situation at hand.

"Thank you all for being here," Billy began, his voice steady despite the turmoil raging within him. "I know that there have been rumours circulating about my personal life, particularly my relationship with Anna. I want to address these rumours head-on and put an end to them once and for all."

With a sense of purpose driving him forward, Billy laid bare the truth of his relationship with Anna, speaking from the heart about the depth of their connection and the unwavering support she had provided him both personally and professionally. As he spoke, a sense of catharsis washed over him, lifting the weight of uncertainty from his shoulders and replacing it with a newfound sense of clarity and resolve.

But while Billy's words resonated with some members of the board, others remained sceptical, their doubts lingering like a dark cloud on the horizon. As the meeting drew to a close, Billy knew that the battle was far from over and that he would need to continue fighting to prove the legitimacy of his relationship with Anna to those who remained unconvinced.

Meanwhile, across town, Anna found herself wrestling with her demons, her fears and insecurities threatening to consume her from within. The strain of hiding her true feelings from Billy weighed heavily on her heart, leaving her feeling isolated and alone in a world that seemed determined to tear them apart.

But amidst the darkness, a glimmer of hope flickered to life within Anna's soul, a reminder that love was worth fighting for, no matter the obstacles that stood in their way. As she summoned the courage to confront her fears head-on, she knew that she couldn't continue to hide behind a facade of strength any longer.

With a deep breath, Anna made her way to Billy's office, her heart pounding in her chest as she prepared to lay bare her soul to the man she loved. As she stood before him, her eyes shining with unshed tears, she knew that this moment would define the course of their future together.

"Billy," Anna began, her voice trembling with emotion. "I need to tell you something."

Billy looked up from his work, his eyes softening at the sight of her. "What is it, Anna?" he asked, his voice gentle yet concerned.

With a shaky breath, Anna spoke the words she had been holding inside for far too long. "I've been struggling, Billy," she confessed, her voice barely above a whisper. "With the rumours, with the pressure, with everything. But most of all, I've been struggling with the fear of losing you."

Billy's heart ached at the pain in Anna's eyes, his own emotions raw and exposed. "Anna, you could never lose me," he vowed, rising from his seat to draw her into his arms. "I love you, more than anything in this world, I will do whatever it takes to prove that to you, every single day for the rest of our lives."

As they held each other close, the weight of their burdens lifted, replaced by a sense of peace and understanding that washed over them like a warm embrace. As they stood together, united in their love and commitment to one another, they knew that no matter what challenges lay ahead, they would face them together, hand in hand, hearts entwined in a bond that could weather any storm.

CHAPTER EIGHT

A NEW BEGINNING

In the wake of their heartfelt confessions, Billy and Anna found themselves standing on the precipice of a new beginning, their love stronger than ever in the face of adversity. With the weight of uncertainty lifted from their shoulders, they embarked on a journey of healing and renewal, determined to forge a path forward together.

As the days turned into weeks, Billy and Anna focused on rebuilding the trust that had been shaken by the rumours surrounding their relationship. They spent long hours in deep conversation, laying bare their fears and insecurities in a bid to strengthen the bond that held them together.

With each passing day, their connection grew deeper, their love blossoming like a flower in the warmth of the sun. They laughed together, cried together, and leaned on each other for support in times of need, their shared experiences weaving the fabric of their relationship into something beautiful and enduring.

Meanwhile, at Billionaire Spikes Housing, Billy redoubled his efforts to quell the rumours that had threatened to undermine his leadership. With the unwavering support of Stanley and the rest of the executive team, he implemented new measures to foster transparency and open communication within the company, ensuring that the voices of all employees were heard and valued.

Slowly but surely, the tide began to turn, and the atmosphere at the company shifted from one of suspicion and mistrust to one of unity and solidarity. As the weeks passed, Billy's reputation as a fair and compassionate leader was restored, and the whispers of doubt that had plagued him began to fade into obscurity.

But amidst the newfound sense of peace and stability, a new challenge emerged on the horizon, one that would test Billy and Anna's resolve like never before. As they stood on the cusp of their happily ever after, a shadow from their past threatened to cast a pall over their future.

It began with a phone call, the shrill ringtone piercing the silence of the night like a dagger through the heart. With a sense of trepidation, Billy reached for the phone, his pulse quickening with each passing moment.

"Hello?" he answered, his voice tinged with uncertainty.

On the other end of the line, a familiar voice spoke, its tone laced with bitterness and resentment. "Billy, it's Milly," the voice said, its words dripping with venom. "I need to talk to you."

Billy's heart sank at the mention of Milly's name, a flood of memories rushing back to him like a tidal wave. He hadn't spoken to her since their time together in school, and the thought of reconnecting with her filled him with a sense of apprehension.

"What is it, Milly?" Billy asked, trying to keep his voice steady despite the turmoil raging within him.

Milly hesitated for a moment before speaking, her words measured and deliberate. "I heard about you and Anna," she said, her voice icy. "And I have some things I need to say."

As Billy listened to Milly's accusations and recriminations, a sense of dread settled over him like a dark cloud on the horizon. He knew that their history together had been fraught with tension and unresolved feelings, and the thought of revisiting those old wounds filled him with a sense of unease.

But amidst the chaos of emotions swirling within him, a voice whispered in the depths of his soul, reminding him that he couldn't ignore the past if he hoped to move forward. And so, with a heavy heart and a sense of determination burning bright within him, Billy made a decision that would change the course of his life forever.

"Meet me tomorrow," he said, his voice firm. "We need to talk."

As Billy hung up the phone, a sense of resolve settled over him like a suit of armour, shielding him from the uncertainty that lay ahead. As he made his way to bed, his mind awash with thoughts of the past and the future, he knew that he was ready to face whatever challenges lay in store, armed with nothing but the strength of his convictions and the love of the woman who held his heart in her hands.

The next day dawned bright and clear, the sun casting its golden rays over the city of Mumbai as Billy made his way to the designated meeting spot. With each step he took, his heart beat a steady rhythm of anticipation, his mind focused on the task at hand.

As he arrived at the appointed location, Billy found Milly waiting for him, her expression guarded yet determined. Without a word, they sat down together, their surroundings fading into the background as they delved into the depths of their shared history.

For hours, they talked, their conversation spanning the breadth of their past grievances and unresolved feelings. As the day wore on, a sense of catharsis washed over them like a cleansing tide, washing away the wounds of the past and paving the way for a new beginning.

By the time they parted ways, Billy felt a weight lifted from his shoulders, a sense of closure settling over him like a warm embrace. As he made his way home to Anna, his heart light with the knowledge that he had faced his demons head-on, he knew that their love was stronger than ever, ready to weather any storm that lay ahead.

As he stepped through the door of their shared apartment, Anna greeted him with a smile, her eyes shining with love and understanding. As they embraced, their hearts beating as one, Billy knew that they were ready to face whatever challenges the future held, hand in hand, united in their love for each other.

For in the end, they knew that love was the greatest gift of all, a beacon of hope in a world filled with darkness, guiding them through the trials and tribulations of life with unwavering strength and grace. As they stood together in the warm glow of the setting sun, they knew that their love would endure for all eternity, a testament to the power of the human heart to overcome even the greatest of obstacles.

As the sun dipped below the horizon, casting a warm golden hue over the city of Mumbai, Billy and Anna found themselves enveloped in a cocoon of love and understanding. The weight of the past lifted from their shoulders, and they embraced the present moment with a renewed sense of purpose and determination.

With Milly's accusations addressed and their past grievances laid to rest, Billy and Anna focused on nurturing their relationship and building a future together. They embarked on new adventures, exploring the vibrant streets of Mumbai hand in hand, their laughter ringing out like music in the night.

But amidst the joy and excitement of their newfound happiness, a sense of unease lingered in the back of their minds, a reminder that life was full of unexpected twists and turns. As they navigated the uncertainties of the present, they couldn't help but wonder what the future held in store for them.

One evening, as they sat together on the balcony of their apartment, watching the stars twinkle overhead, Billy broached the subject that had been weighing on his mind.

"Anna," he began, his voice soft yet serious. "I've been thinking about our future, about what comes next for us."

Anna turned to him, her eyes filled with curiosity. "What do you mean, Billy?" she asked, her heart racing with anticipation.

Billy took a deep breath, gathering his thoughts before speaking. "I want us to build a life together, Anna," he said, his voice filled with conviction. "I want to wake up next to you every morning, to share our hopes and dreams, our triumphs and challenges. I want us to create a future that's brighter and more beautiful than anything we could ever imagine."

Anna's heart swelled with emotion at Billy's words, her eyes shining with tears of joy. "Oh, Billy," she whispered, her voice choked with emotion. "I want that too, more than anything in this world."

As they held each other close, their love burning bright like a beacon in the night, they knew that their future was filled with endless possibilities, their hearts united in a bond that could withstand even the greatest of storms.

But as they embraced the promise of tomorrow, a new challenge emerged on the horizon, one that would test their resolve and push them to their limits. Unbeknownst to them, a shadow from their past lurked in the shadows, waiting to strike when they least expected it.

It began with a letter, delivered to their doorstep in the dead of night, its contents a harbinger of doom that sent shivers down their spines. With trembling hands, Billy tore open the envelope, his heart pounding in his chest as he read the words written on the page.

"Dear Billy and Anna," the letter began, its tone cold and menacing. "I know what you've done, and I won't rest until you pay for your sins. You may think you've escaped the past, but it's only a matter of time before it catches up to you. Beware, for the darkness is coming, and there's nowhere left to hide."

As Billy and Anna read the ominous words, a sense of dread washed over them like a tidal wave, threatening to engulf them in its icy grip. They knew that they couldn't ignore the threat looming on the horizon, that they would need to confront it head-on if they hoped to protect the life they had built together.

With a shared sense of determination burning bright within them, Billy and Anna vowed to face whatever challenges lay ahead, united in their love and steadfast in their resolve. For they knew that no matter what trials they faced, as long as they had each other, they could weather any storm and emerge stronger on the other side.

And so, as they stood together on the balcony of their apartment, their hands clasped tight and their hearts filled with hope, they braced themselves for the battles yet to come, ready to fight for their love with every ounce of strength they possessed. For in the end, they knew that love was the greatest weapon of all, a force more powerful than any darkness that dared to stand in its way.

<u>CONFRONTING THE SHADOWS</u>

As the ominous words of the letter echoed in their minds, Billy and Anna found themselves thrust into a world of uncertainty and fear. The threat of the past loomed large over their heads, casting a shadow over their once peaceful existence.

With a sense of urgency burning within them, Billy and Anna wasted no time in springing into action. They knew that they couldn't afford to ignore the warning contained in the letter, that they needed to confront the darkness head-on if they hoped to protect the life they had built together.

Their first step was to seek guidance from those they trusted most. They reached out to TeaBag and Stacy, sharing the contents of the letter and enlisting their help in unravelling the mystery of its origins.

TeaBag's face darkened with concern as he read the letter, his mind racing with thoughts of possible suspects and motives. "This doesn't sound like idle threats," he said, his voice grave. "We need to take this seriously."

Stacy nodded in agreement, her expression mirroring TeaBag's concern. "We'll do whatever it takes to keep you safe," she vowed, her voice resolute. "But we need to tread carefully. We don't know who we're dealing with."

With their friends by their side, Billy and Anna set out to uncover the truth behind the menacing letter. They combed through their pasts with a fine-toothed comb, searching for any clues that might shed light on the identity of their mysterious assailant.

But despite their best efforts, the answers remained elusive, hidden behind a veil of secrecy and deception. With each dead end they encountered, their frustration grew, threatening to overwhelm them in a tidal wave of despair.

As the days turned into weeks, the weight of the unknown bore down upon them like a heavy burden, casting a pall over their once bright and hopeful future. As they struggled to make sense of the chaos swirling around them, they couldn't help but wonder if they would ever find the answers they so desperately sought.

But just when all hope seemed lost, a breakthrough came in the most unexpected of places. It began with a chance encounter on the bustling streets of Mumbai, where Billy and Anna found themselves face to face with a figure from their past they had long since forgotten.

It was Milly, her eyes filled with remorse as she approached them tentatively. "Billy, Anna," she began, her voice quavering with emotion. "I need to talk to you."

Billy and Anna exchanged a puzzled glance, unsure of what to make of Milly's sudden appearance. But something in her demeanour told them that this was no chance encounter, that she had something important to share with them.

With a sense of trepidation, they followed Milly to a nearby café, where they sat down together in a secluded corner away from prying eyes. As Milly began to speak, her words sent shockwaves through the air, shattering the fragile peace they had fought so hard to maintain.

"I know who sent the letter," Milly confessed, her voice barely above a whisper. "It was me."

Billy and Anna's hearts stopped in their chests as the weight of Milly's words sank in. They couldn't believe what they were hearing, couldn't fathom that someone they had once trusted could betray them in such a cruel manner.

"Why, Milly?" Anna asked, her voice tinged with disbelief. "Why would you do something like this?"

Milly hung her head in shame, unable to meet their gaze. "I was jealous," she admitted, her words choked with emotion. "Jealous of the life you two had built together, of the love you shared. I wanted to tear it all apart, to see you suffer like I had suffered."

Billy and Anna sat in stunned silence, the enormity of Milly's betrayal washing over them like a tidal wave. They couldn't comprehend how someone they had once considered a friend could harbour such malice and resentment towards them.

But amidst the chaos of their emotions, a sense of clarity began to emerge. They realized that the true enemy wasn't Milly herself, but the darkness that had consumed her heart and led her down a path of destruction.

With a heavy heart, Billy reached out and took Milly's hand in his, his voice filled with compassion and forgiveness. "Milly," he said, his words a balm to her wounded soul. "We may never understand why you did what you did, but we forgive you. We believe that there's still goodness in your heart, that you can find redemption if you're willing to seek it."

Milly's eyes filled with tears at Billy's words, her heart heavy with remorse for the pain she had caused. "Thank you," she whispered, her voice trembling with emotion. "I don't deserve your forgiveness, but I promise to do everything in my power to make amends for what I've done."

And so, with the weight of the truth laid bare and forgiveness granted, Billy, Anna, and Milly embarked on a journey of healing and reconciliation. They knew that the road ahead would be long and fraught with challenges, but they faced it together, united in their determination to overcome the darkness that had threatened to tear them apart.

As they walked hand in hand through the streets of Mumbai, the weight of the past lifted from their shoulders, they felt a sense of peace wash over them like a gentle breeze. As they looked towards the horizon, their hearts filled with hope for the future, they knew that no matter what trials lay ahead, they would face them with courage, strength, and love. For in the end, they knew that love was the greatest force in the universe, capable of conquering even the darkest of shadows and lighting the way to a brighter tomorrow.

With the weight of the truth finally revealed and forgiveness extended, Billy, Anna, and Milly embarked on a journey of reconciliation and redemption. They understood that healing would take time, but they were determined to move forward together, armed with the strength of their newfound understanding and forgiveness.

As they navigated the weeks that followed, Billy, Anna, and Milly engaged in honest and open conversations, addressing the wounds of the past and laying the foundation for a brighter future. They shared their hopes, fears, and dreams, forging a bond of friendship that transcended the pain and betrayal that had once threatened to tear them apart.

With each passing day, the darkness that had consumed Milly's heart began to dissipate, replaced by a newfound sense of purpose and compassion. She threw herself into acts of kindness and service, seeking to atone for the pain she had caused and make amends for her past mistakes.

Meanwhile, Billy and Anna focused on strengthening their relationship, cherishing each moment they shared and building a future filled with love, laughter, and endless possibilities. They knew that their journey was far from over, but they faced the challenges ahead with a sense of hope and optimism, secure in the knowledge that they had each other to lean on.

As the days turned into months, Billy, Anna, and Milly found themselves drawn together by a bond that transcended the trials and tribulations of the past. They laughed together, cried together, and celebrated each other's victories, their friendship a beacon of light in a world that often seemed dark and uncertain.

But amidst the joy and camaraderie, a shadow from their past lingered in the shadows, waiting for an opportunity to strike when they least expected it. It came in the form of a mysterious figure, lurking in the shadows and plotting their downfall with ruthless precision.

One fateful evening, as Billy, Anna, and Milly gathered for dinner at their favourite restaurant, they were confronted by the sinister presence of their unknown adversary. With a sense of dread twisting in their stomachs, they watched in horror as the figure emerged from the darkness, his face obscured by a mask of malice and deceit.

"Hello, Billy," the figure hissed, his voice dripping with venom. "I see you've made some new friends. Too bad they won't be around for long."

Billy's heart raced as he faced the shadowy figure, his mind racing with thoughts of how to protect Anna and Milly from the danger that lurked in their midst. With a steely resolve, he stepped forward, shielding them from harm with his own body.

"Who are you?" Billy demanded, his voice filled with defiance. "And what do you want from us?"

The figure laughed, a cold, mocking sound that sent shivers down their spines. "You think you can stop me, Billy?" he sneered. "You're nothing but a pawn in my game, a pawn that's about to be taken off the board."

With a swift movement, the figure lunged forward, his intentions clear as he reached for Billy with outstretched hands. But before he could make contact, a blur of motion streaked through the air, knocking him off balance and sending him crashing to the ground.

As the figure struggled to regain his footing, Billy, Anna, and Milly looked on in shock as a familiar face emerged from the shadows, his eyes burning with determination.

It was TeaBag, his fists clenched and his jaw set in a fierce expression of resolve. "You picked the wrong people to mess with," he growled, his voice low and menacing. "Now get out of here before things get ugly."

With a defeated scowl, the figure slunk back into the darkness, disappearing into the night like a ghostly spectre. As Billy, Anna, Milly, and TeaBag stood together in the aftermath of the confrontation, they knew that they had faced their greatest challenge yet and emerged victorious, united in their determination to protect each other at all costs.

As they made their way home, the weight of the encounter still heavy on their hearts, Billy, Anna, Milly, and TeaBag found solace in the knowledge that they were stronger together than they ever could have been apart. As they looked towards the future with hope and optimism, they knew that no matter what trials lay ahead, they would face them with courage, strength, and love, secure in the knowledge that they had each other to lean on. For in the end, they knew that together, they could overcome any obstacle and emerge stronger on the other side.

CHAPTER TEN

<u>EMBRACING THE FUTURE</u>

In the wake of their harrowing encounter with the shadowy figure, Billy, Anna, Milly, and TeaBag found themselves grappling with a renewed sense of urgency. The threat of danger still loomed large over their heads, casting a shadow of uncertainty over their once-peaceful existence.

Determined to protect each other and their loved ones, they banded together with a newfound sense of purpose, rallying around the bonds of friendship and camaraderie that had sustained them through the darkest of times.

With their hearts filled with determination and their minds focused on the task at hand, they set out to uncover the identity of their mysterious adversary and put an end to the threat once and for all.

Their journey led them down a twisting path of secrets and lies, as they delved deep into the underbelly of Mumbai's criminal underworld in search of answers. With each new clue they uncovered, their resolve only strengthened, fueling their determination to bring the truth to light and ensure that justice was served.

But as they delved deeper into the shadows, they soon realized that their adversary was more cunning and elusive than they had ever imagined. With every step they took, he seemed to slip through their fingers like a wisp of smoke, leaving nothing but confusion and frustration in his wake.

Despite the setbacks and obstacles they faced, Billy, Anna, Milly, and TeaBag refused to be deterred. They knew that they couldn't afford to give up and that the safety of their loved ones depended on their ability to confront the darkness head-on and emerge victorious.

And so, with a renewed sense of determination burning bright within them, they redoubled their efforts, leaving no stone unturned in their quest for the truth. They sought out allies in unexpected places, forging alliances with those who shared their desire for justice and their commitment to protecting the innocent.

As the days turned into weeks and the weeks turned into months, their perseverance finally paid off, as they uncovered a crucial piece of evidence that would lead them straight to the heart of the mystery.

It was a photograph, hidden away in a dusty file deep within the archives of the Mumbai Police Department. In it, they saw the face of their adversary staring back at them with a cold, steely gaze, his identity finally revealed.

With the truth laid bare before them, Billy, Anna, Milly, and TeaBag knew that the time for action had come. Armed with the evidence they needed to bring their adversary to justice, they set out to confront him once and for all, determined to put an end to the threat that had loomed over their lives for far too long.

Their journey led them to a deserted warehouse on the outskirts of the city, where they found themselves face-to-face with their adversary at last. With a sense of grim determination, they squared their shoulders and prepared for the battle ahead, knowing that the outcome would determine the fate of their future.

As the confrontation unfolded, tensions ran high, the air thick with anticipation and fear. But amidst the chaos and uncertainty, a sense of unity and purpose emerged, binding Billy, Anna, Milly, and TeaBag together for a common cause.

With each blow they struck and each obstacle they overcame, they drew closer to victory, their determination unshakable in the face of adversity. As the showdown reached its climax, they fought with everything they had, their hearts burning bright with the fire of justice and righteousness.

In the end, it was their unwavering commitment to each other and their shared belief in the power of love and friendship that carried them through. With a final, decisive blow, they vanquished their adversary once and for all, ensuring that he could never again threaten the peace and safety of their lives.

As they emerged victorious from the fray, battered but unbroken, Billy, Anna, Milly, and TeaBag knew that their journey was far from over. But as they looked towards the horizon with hope and optimism, they knew that they faced the future together, stronger and more united than ever before.

For in the end, they learned that no matter what trials and tribulations they faced, as long as they stood together, they could overcome any obstacle and emerge victorious. As they embraced the promise of tomorrow with open arms, they knew that their love and friendship would light the way, guiding them through even the darkest of nights towards a brighter, more hopeful future.

As the dust settled and the adrenaline of the confrontation began to ebb away, Billy, Anna, Milly, and TeaBag found themselves standing amidst the remnants of their battle, their hearts heavy with both relief and exhaustion. They had emerged victorious, but the toll of their struggle was evident in the weariness etched into their faces.

With a shared sense of relief washing over them, they exchanged weary smiles and clasped hands, their bond stronger than ever in the wake of their triumph. For in the crucible of adversity, they had forged a connection that transcended the boundaries of friendship, uniting them in a shared purpose and a common cause.

But amidst the sense of victory, a sense of uncertainty lingered in the air, a reminder that their journey was far from over. They knew that the road ahead would be fraught with challenges and obstacles, but they faced it with a sense of determination and resolve born from their shared experiences.

As they made their way back to the safety of their homes, they were met with a sense of relief and gratitude from their loved ones, who had waited anxiously for news of their fate. Their families and friends enveloped them in warm embraces, their eyes shining with tears of joy and relief at their safe return.

For Billy and Anna, the ordeal had brought them closer together than ever before, reaffirming the strength of their love and the depth of their commitment to each other. They knew that no matter what trials lay ahead, as long as they had each other, they could weather any storm and emerge stronger on the other side.

As they settled back into the rhythms of their daily lives, Billy, Anna, Milly, and TeaBag found themselves grappling with the aftermath of their ordeal, each grappling with their demons and insecurities in the wake of their shared trauma.

But amidst the darkness, a sense of hope began to bloom within their hearts, a reminder that even in the darkest of times, there was always light to be found. They leaned on each other for support, drawing strength from the bonds of friendship and camaraderie that had sustained them through the darkest of nights.

As they looked towards the future with hope and optimism, they knew that they had emerged from their trials stronger and more resilient than ever before. For in the crucible of adversity, they had discovered the true power of love and friendship, and they knew that as long as they stood together, they could overcome any obstacle that stood in their way.

As they watched the sun set on another day, casting its warm golden rays over the city of Mumbai, Billy, Anna, Milly, and TeaBag stood together on the balcony of their apartment, their hearts filled with gratitude for the journey that had brought them to this moment.

In the end, they knew that it was their shared experiences and their unwavering commitment to each other that had carried them through the darkest of times, guiding them towards a future filled with hope, promise, and endless possibility. As they embraced the promise of tomorrow with open arms, they knew that no matter what trials and tribulations lay ahead, they would face them together, united in their love and friendship, forever and always.

Farewell For Now

Thank you for embarking on this journey into the heart of Mumbai with "The Young Billionaire." As we come to the close of this captivating tale, I extend my deepest gratitude to you, dear reader, for your support, your curiosity, and your willingness to immerse yourself in the lives of Billy and his friends.

But as the final pages turn and we bid farewell to our beloved characters, let us remember that the story does not end here. For just as Billy's journey continues beyond these words, so too does ours. May the lessons learned, the friendships forged, and the dreams pursued within these pages inspire you to chase your own dreams with courage, determination, and unwavering belief in the power of love and friendship.

As you close this book and return to the world outside, may you carry with you the spirit of adventure, the resilience of the human spirit, and the knowledge that no dream is too big, no obstacle too daunting, and no journey too perilous when embarked upon with an open heart and a steadfast resolve.

Until we meet again, dear reader, may your days be filled with laughter, love, and the boundless possibility of tomorrow.

With warm regards,
Cwebile Ndebele (B.S)

www.ingramcontent.com/pod-product-compliance
Lightning Source LLC
Chambersburg PA
CBHW022118150726
47990CB00003B/1412